Isaiah 26:3 - 4
"Perfect Peace XVII"

Arrow

VANESSA RAYNER

authorHOUSE®

AuthorHouse™
1663 Liberty Drive
Bloomington, IN 47403
www.authorhouse.com
Phone: 1 (800) 839-8640

Published by AuthorHouse 01/25/2019

ISBN: 978-1-5462-7775-0 (sc)
ISBN: 978-1-5462-7774-3 (e)

Library of Congress Control Number: 2019900931

Print information available on the last page.

CONTENTS

A GIFT . . .

$P_{resented\ to}$

_____

F_{rom}

_____

D_{ate}

_____

God is the Author of Possibilities;
who specializes in impossibilities!

THEME

The message of **Isaiah 26:3-4** is "Perfect Peace." This is the distinct and unifying composition of this book with the subtitle **Arrow**.

<u>A Song of Praise</u>
You will keep in perfect peace those
whose minds are steadfast,
Trust in the Lord forever, for the Lord, the
Lord himself, is the Rock eternal.
Isaiah 26:3-4 NIV

PRAYER

Oh, Heavenly Father,
I thank you for another day.
I thank you for another opportunity
to write another book.
Hallelujah!
I pray that your people are being enlightened
and encouraged, everywhere.

Oh, Heavenly Father,
I ask in Jesus' name that the Holy Spirit will
help readers to remember Your word.
I pray the word of God will give them
peace when they need it the most.
I thank you, Father, for blessing those
that help Your work go forth.

Oh, Heavenly Father,
Your word made it clear that You will
reward those that bless your servant.
It could be through prayer, words of encouragement,
to giving that person a cup of water.

Mark 9:41 says,
If anyone gives you even a cup of water
because you belong to the Messiah,
I tell you the truth, that person will
surely be rewarded; NLT.

Oh, Father God,
I give you all the Glory, Honor and Praise,
in Jesus' name.
Amen.

AUTHOR'S NOTES

Author notes generally provide a way to add extra information to one's book that may be awkward and inappropriate to include in the text of the book itself. It offers supplemental contextual details on the aspects of the book. It can help readers understand the book content and the background details of the book better. The times and dates of researching, reading, and gathering this information are not included; mostly when I typed on it.

1705; Wednesday, 24 October 2018
1653; Wednesday, 31 October 2018
1642; Friday, 02 November 2018
0647; Saturday, 03 November 2018
0844; Sunday, 04 November 2018
1733; Monday, 05 November 2018
1645; Tuesday, 06 November 2018; This morning at 0722, I was praying in my kitchen. In the prayer I asked, Father God why am I constantly waking up throughout the night, starting at midnight? Suddenly, I begin to hear the lyrics "In The Midnight Hour" by Wilson Pickett . . . smile; that's what I did. Then the lyrics of Lee Williams & The Spiritual QC song titled "In The Midnight Hour" came to

me. I hummed it all day at work; sounds like a book title to me. Hallelujah!

1711; Wednesday, 07 November 2018

1642; Thursday, 08 November 2018

1732; Friday, 09 November 2018

0621; Sunday, 11 November 2018

0733; Monday, 12 November 2018; Happy Veteran Day!

1752; Tuesday, 13 November 2018

1652; Thursday, 15 November 2018

1632; Friday, 16 November 2018

0705; Saturday, 17 November 2018

0805; Sunday, 18 November 2018

1649; Monday, 19 November 2018

1618; Tuesday, 20 November 2018

1444; Wednesday, 21 November 2018; Home early today, waiting on a Sears Technician to come, and repair my Kenmore Ice Dispenser. Praise God in spike of!

0504; Thursday, 22 November 2018; Happy Thanksgiving!

0453; Friday, 23 November 2018

0000; Saturday, 24 November 2018

0519; Sunday, 25 November 2018

1854; Monday, 26 November 2018

1438; Tuesday, 27 November 2018

1657; Wednesday, 28 November 2018

1637; Thursday, 29 November 2018

1653; Friday, 30 November 2018

0515; Saturday, 01 December 2018

0639; Sunday, 02 December 2018; Tell me what you want. . . Tell me what you need . . . Anything is possible. . . Tell me what you want. . . I will understand . . . No requests are going unheard . . . Woke up this morning with these words playing in my head with Dru Hill's music beat. Hallelujah!

1632; Monday, 03 December 2018

2211; Tuesday, 04 December 2018

1637; Wednesday, 05 December 2018

1709; Thursday, 06 December 2018

1739; Friday, 07 December 2018

0900; Saturday, 08 December 2018

0753; Sunday, 09 December 2018

1630; Monday, 10 December 2018

1704; Wednesday, 12 December 2018

1623; Thursday, 13 December 2018

1720; Friday, 14 December 2018

0753; Saturday, 15 December 2018

0621; Sunday, 16 December 2018

1628; Monday, 17 December 2018

1942; Wednesday, 19 December 2018

1628; Thursday, 20 December 2018

1620; Friday, 21 December 2018; "Luke 2" – I'm schedule to speak on Pastor JoAnn's Breaking Bread Fellowship Prayer Line at 1900 hours. Praise God!

0744; Saturday, 22 December 2018

0736; Sunday, 23 December 2018

0538; Monday, 24 December 2018

0638; Tuesday, 25 December 2018: Merry Christmas!

1704; Wednesday, 26 December 2018

1628; Thursday, 27 December 2018

1709; Friday; 28 December 2018

0526; Saturday, 29 December 2018

1118; Sunday, 30 December 2018

0655; Monday, 31 December 2018

0156; Tuesday, 01 January 2019; Happy New Year! Lord I Thank You . . .

1632; Wednesday, 02 January 2019

1628; Thursday, 03 January 2019

1628; Friday, 04 January 2019

0544; Saturday, 05 January 2019

0723; Sunday, 06 January 2019

2029; Monday, 07 January 2019; Severe back pain on the right-side which started Sunday evening, sent me to the Doctor, this morning. Just took my meds for the issue. I'm going to look over and type on this book until the sleep hits me. Hallelujah to the Most Highest!

0041; Tuesday, 08 January 2019

0716; Wednesday, 09 January 2019; A beautiful scene: I'm setting in my favorite chair about to work on this book, looking out the front door that faces east, and the Sun is rising. It's so, so, so bright, even though, I can't look directly at it; I can feel the warmth and love from it. I had to move over in my chair to the left a little so that the door frame could block some of the rays of the Sun brightness. . . That's how the Shekinah Glory must be. Praise God! As I'm typing at 0721 most of the rays of the Sun just got cover by the edge of a building at the corner of the next street over. Hallelujah! Now at 0737, the full Sun is rising above the building that once blocked the rays. I got up and pushed the door almost closed, but the rays of the **Son** are still beaming through the slightly open door. Amazing . . .

1525; Friday, 11 January 2019

0712; Saturday, 12 January 2019

0627; Sunday, 13 January 2019

1616; Monday, 14 January 2019

1631; Tuesday, 15 January 2019

1753; Wednesday, 16 January 2019; I'm going to read over a page or two until it's time to go to Kevin B. Well, International Faith Covenant Fellowship Prayer Line at 1800; CST.

1633; Thursday, 17 January 2019

1823; Tuesday, 22 January 2019; In an hour or so, I will be emailing the manuscript to AuthorHouse. Hallelujah!

PREFACE
THANKS

Isaiah 26:3-4, "Perfect Peace XVII" Arrow

The book <u>Isaiah 26:3-4, "Perfect Peace XVII" Arrow</u> is the 17th book in a series called Isaiah 26:3-4, "Perfect Peace." Hallelujah!

It all started from how I drew near to the LORD in my workplace by keeping my mind on Him. I related numbers you see throughout the day, everywhere, on almost everything on Him, His word, biblical events, and facts to give me peace in the midst of chaos.

It's our desire for you to discover the power of the Holy Spirit by numbers, words, places, people, and things related to the word "arrow."

Remember, the LORD Jesus <u>PROMISED us tribulation</u> while we were in this world.

These things, I have spoken unto you,
that in me ye might have peace.
In the world ye shall have tribulation:
But be of good cheer; I have overcome the world.
John 16:33 KJV

However, we have been <u>PROMISED His peace</u> while we endure these trials, tribulations, troubles, and tests. Perfect Peace is given only to those whose mind and heart reclines upon the LORD. God's peace is increased in us according to the knowledge of His Holy Word.

Grace and peace be multiplied unto you
through the knowledge of God,
and of Jesus our LORD.
2 Peter 1:2 KJV

To The Readers of The World

As a disciple of the LORD Jesus Christ, I have learned true success comes when we are seeking and striving to do God's purpose for our lives. Our real happiness lies in doing God's will; not in fame and fortune.

I appreciate your support. Thanks for helping me spread "Perfect Peace" through your e-mail, Facebook, Twitter, LinkedIn, Instagram, Tumblr, Messenger and or other accounts to your family, friends, neighbors, co-workers, church family, internet social friends, and associates.

Remember, you may not know until you get to heaven just how much a song you sung, kind words spoken by you or even a book you suggested reading, at the right moment, encourage a person to keep on going when a few minutes before they were tempted to give up on life and their walk with the LORD.

Your lovingkindness to this ministry is greatly appreciate.

ACKNOWLEDGEMENTS

I wish to express my sincere gratitude to *"Our Heavenly Father"* for his guidance, patience, and lovingkindness throughout the writing of this book.

I thank all whose prayers, encouraging words, research, and support helped me to write this book.

INTRODUCTION

For Those Who Want to Be Kept In "Perfect Peace"

This book was prepared and written to open your mind to a "Perfect Peace" that comes only from God. I'm striving to elevate you into a "Unique and Profound" awareness of God's presence around you at all time.

According to some people, it's hard to keep your mind on the LORD. While most Christians will agree that if you keep your mind stayed on the LORD, He will keep you in "Perfect Peace." This is why so many people enjoy going to church on Sundays and attending midweek services for peace and joy that they receive, but only for a short time.

You can experience the peace of the LORD throughout the day and every day. His unspeakable joy, his strength, his "Perfect Peace" in the midst of the storm whether it's at work, home, college, school, etc. You can also experience this peace, even when your day is going well.

This concept of this book was placed in my spirit by our Father, which art in heaven, to help me when he allowed Satan to test me at my workplace until he finished molding me into a MAP; (Minister/Ambassador/Pastor).

Throughout these pages, I will be focussing on biblical events, and facts surrounding the word "arrow." However, I am sure much more can be said concerning the word "arrow" in the Bible, so these subjects serve merely as an introduction and are not exhaustive by any means.

DEDICATION

All the Lover of Archery
The Bowyers
The Fletchers
The Arrowsmith
The Bowman/Archers
The Toxophilite

CHAPTER 1

Arrow

An arrow is described as a long slender pointed projectile that can be used as a weapon, for hunting or in a competitive sport. An arrow consists of a long straight shaft, fletches, a sharply pointed arrowhead attached to the front end, and a slot at the rear end called the nock.

A craftsman who makes arrows is called a "Fletcher." He is called a "Fletcher" because of the small feathers at the end of the arrow that is called "fletches." They are bound to the arrow's shaft, and they help stabilize the flight of the arrow while keeping the arrow pointed in the direction of travel. Fletches were traditionally made from goose or turkey feathers. In Bible days, "fletches" were known as "the tail" and were made from feathers of eagle, vulture, or seabirds. Now, fletches are made from a plastic known as vanes.

A person who makes the arrowheads of the arrow is called an "Arrowsmith." The arrowhead also known as the projectile point is part of the arrow that plays the most significant role in its purpose; weapon, hunting, sport. Arrowheads were

1

usually made from metal, horn, bone, or some other hard material in Bible days. Most arrowheads were shaped like a leaf, and some were made triangular and flat.

In the Middle Ages, there were 2 basic types of arrows called broadhead/barbed and bodkin/non-barbed. The broadhead arrows were used mostly against unarmored individuals. The bodkin type arrows were war arrows meant to be used against armored individuals.

Note of Interests: The Middle Ages lasted approximately 1000 years; 5th to 15th BC. It began at the fall of the Western Roman Empire in the 5th BC and lasted until the beginning of the Renaissance in the 15th BC. The Dark Ages are referred to the initial 500 years of the Middle Ages. During this time, it was raided by the barbarians from northern and central Europe, and the people suffered from hunger and were plagued with many diseases.

The shaft is the fundamental part of the arrow in which the other components are attached. Traditionally, arrow shafts were made from durable wood, bamboo or reeds. A nock is a notch at the tail-end of an arrow shaft that is used for engaging the bowstring. It helps keep the arrow from slipping sideways during the draw or after the release of the arrow. The primary purpose of the nock is to control the rotation of the arrow.

A varnish type material would be applied to the arrows so that they are not softened by rain. In time, crests rings of color paint were painted on arrows to indicate the owner of the arrow.

The use of an arrow by humanity was common in most cultures. The bow and arrow were the primary weapons in all the battles mentioned in the Bible. It had an effective range of about 400 yards. The arrows were generally carried in a long quiver made of animal hides to protect them. Today, there are many different makes, models, brands, and types of bows and arrows with specific names and purposes.

During the kingdoms of Israel and Judah, archers played a crucial part in battles. They were prestige warriors trained to shoot arrows against cities and in open terrain. When engaged in combat, they needed both of their hands to use the bow and arrow. They wore a long coat of armor for body protection and was accompanied by a shield-bearer, who held a small round shield to protect the archer's face.

Note of Interests: The tribe of Benjamin was well-known for the use of the bow, along with the Elamites and Lydians, 1 Chronicles 8:40, 1 Chronicles 12:2, Isaiah 22:6, and Jeremiah 46:9. Psalm 120:4, mentions that arrows were sometimes shot with flaming hot coals attached to them.

Tiglath-Pileser, an Assyrian king created a more massive shield that was long and heavy which was carried by a shield-bearer to cover the archer. The shield was made longer than the height of the man, and the top of the shield was angled, like a hood that curved inward, to shield the archer from the arrows of the soldiers on a wall.

However, the earliest evidence of stone-tipped arrowheads dates to 64,000 years ago. It was discovered in Sibudu Cave located in South Africa. The oldest evidence of the use of a bow to shoot arrows dates to 10,000 years ago. Pinewood arrows that had shallow grooves on the base of the arrow were found in the Ahrensburg Valley north of Hamburg in German. These arrows were most likely shot from a bow.

The word "arrow" is an uncommon word used in the Old English language; the West Germanic language. A more common word for "arrow" was "strael." The word "strael" was once common in Germanic that relates to the words meaning "flash."

Note of Interests: The Old English language is also called Anglo-Saxon. It was a language spoken and written in an area that is now England and Southern Scotland between 5th and 12th century. Old English is the ancestor of Middle English and Modern English. The West Germanic languages are English, Frisian, Dutch, Afrikaans, German, and Yiddish. The North Germanic languages are Danish, Faroese, Icelandic, Norwegian and Swedish.

The words "fla, flan" are other common words for "arrow" from Old Norse, a North Germanic word which is believed to have originated from a "splinter." The word "strael" for arrow disappeared by 1200 AD, and the word "fla" became "flo" in the early Middle English, and slowly disappeared in Scottish around 1500 AD.

The words "arrow" and "arrows" are only found in the Old Testament, KJV. The word "arrow" is mentioned 14 times in 9 books of the Bible which are 1 Samuel, 2 Kings, Job, Psalm, Proverbs, Isaiah, Jeremiah, Lamentations, and Zechariah.

Old Testament

Historical Books
1 Samuel 20:36
1 Samuel 20:37
2 Kings 9:24
2 Kings 13:17
2 Kings 19:32

The Poetic Books
Job 41:28
Psalm 11:2
Psalm 64:7
Psalm 91:5
Proverbs 25:18

Major Prophet Books
Isaiah 37:33
Jeremiah 9:8
Lamentations 3:12

Minor Prophet Book
Zechariah 9:14

CHAPTER 2

The Stone Ezel

The stone named "Ezel" was a stone located outside the city where Saul lived, 1 Samuel 20:19. The word "Ezel" means "departure," and it is only mentioned once in the Bible. The stone Ezel was well-known to Jonathan and David in Bible days. The exact location of the stone is unknown, today. Some Scholars believe Ezel was a stone set-up beside a road or area to mark the distance which directed travelers.

The stone Ezel is where David hid, waiting for Jonathan to come and shoot arrows toward it. This action by Jonathan would serve as a signal to David, whether to stay or flee from King Saul. The stone Ezel is also where David and Jonathan said their goodbyes in sadness.

Beginning at 1 Samuel 18:6, an incident prompted Saul's jealousy of David. It was after Saul and David returned to Gibeah after the pursuit and slaughter of the Philistines. The women came out of the cities of Israel to meet King Saul. The women were dancing, playing their tambourines, harps and cymbals and sang to one another, "Saul has slain his thousands, and David his tens of thousands," 1 Samuel 18:7. Saul became enraged, and afterward on several occasions, attempted to take David's life.

After they returned to the palace, David was playing his harp for the king, as usual, when suddenly Saul threw his javelin at his head, intending to kill him. David avoided the thrust of the weapon and hastened out of the king's presence. Saul removed David from his household. He made David the captain over 1,000 soldiers. King Saul was hoping that the dangers of war would result in David's death.

David's military triumphs became great in number, and the people were excited. Saul's jealousy grew into hatred. Once more Saul tried to kill David, and it was only on the appeal of his son, Jonathan that King Saul refrained. King Saul even restore harmony with David, but the friendly relationship with David didn't last long, 1 Samuel 19:1 – 8.

Another war broke out against the Philistines and the Israelites. David led the troops, and they were victorious. Afterward, Saul envy rose again. Days later, David was playing his harp for Saul, and suddenly Saul in a fit of rage attempted to slay David with his javelin, again. David escaped into the night, 1 Samuel 19:8 – 10.

David sought refuge in his own house with his wife, Michal. He was followed by the king's messengers, who were ordered to kill him. Michal, the daughter of Saul, fearing for her husband's life, helped him escape through a window. David fled to Naioth in Ramah to see Samuel, but he only stayed there a short time, 1 Samuel 19:11 – 18.

The word "arrow" is mentioned in the 20th chapter of 1 Samuel which has 42 verses. The word "arrow" without the "s" is mentioned 3 times in verses 36 and 37 of this chapter; twice in verse 37, KJV.

In the morning Jonathan went out to the field
for his meeting with David. He had a small
boy with him, and he said to the boy,
"Run and find the arrows I shoot."
As the boy ran, he shot an arrow beyond him.
When the boy came to the place where
Jonathan's arrow had fallen, Jonathan called
out after him, "Isn't the arrow beyond you?"
1 Samuel 20:35 – 37 NIV

According to 1 Samuel 20:1 – 2, David fears for his life because Saul, the King of Israel is trying to kill him. David goes to his best friend, Jonathan, the king's son, and asked why.

Jonathan tries to ensure David that his father, the king has no intention of killing him. Jonathan tells David that his father tells him everything. David reminds Jonathan that Saul knows of their friendship and therefore, wouldn't tell him, he was plotting to kill him. Jonathan tells David he will do whatever he can to help him, 1 Samuel 20:3 – 4.

David tells Jonathan, he is supposed to have dinner with Saul tomorrow at the New Moon Festival, but he will be hiding in the fields until the day after the festival. David asks Jonathan to tell Saul; he had to hurry to Bethlehem for a sacrifice. David tells Jonathan, if Saul doesn't get angry, then he is safe to be in King Saul's presence, but if he becomes angry that means Saul is determined to kill him, 1 Samuel 20:5 – 11.

According to 1 Samuel 20:12 – 23, David and Jonathan went into the field. There Jonathan tells David that he will let him know Saul's disposition towards him. They pledge their friendship and Jonathan tells David to wait by the stone called Ezel.

Jonathan tells David, he will shoot arrows as though he was shooting at a target. He will say to the boy find the arrows. If he tells his servant, "You went too far! The arrows are closer to me, come back and get them." David can come out of hiding, but if he tells the servant boy "the arrows are farther away!" This would mean that David's life is in danger and he need to flee.

When it was time for the New Moon Festival, David didn't appear. Saul thought that David was probably ritually unclean. David didn't show up the next evening, and Saul asked Jonathan about David. Jonathan then tells his father he allowed David to go sacrifice in Bethlehem, 1 Samuel 20:24 – 29.

Saul becomes enraged. He demanded that David is brought back at once to be killed. Jonathan demands to know why, but his father only throws a spear at him, 1 Samuel 20:30 – 32.

Note of Interests: The New Moon Festival in the Old Testament is when the Jews visited the Temple of Jerusalem with a special sacrifice. Each new month in the year was consecrated to God, and it was marked by the blowing of trumpets over the sacrifices, abstaining from all labor with a feast gathering, Numbers 10:10, Nehemiah 10:31, 1 Samuel 20:5. The observance of the New Moon Festival is no longer required. The perfect sacrifice of God appeared, and He rendered the observation of this ordinance no longer necessary. Jesus Christ fulfilled all the righteous requirements of the Law by His work on the cross, Matthew 5:17 and Colossians 2:16 – 17.

Early, the next morning, Jonathan goes to the field with his servant. He shoots the arrows, and shout to the servant boy that the arrows are beyond him, and David knows he must flee. Jonathan gives his servants the arrows and tells him to go back to town. When the boy is gone, David comes out of hiding. Jonathan and David kissed each other and wept. David flees for his safety, and Jonathan returns to his father's palace, 1 Samuel 20:35 – 42.

Question: How many arrows did Jonathan shoot? *smile*

Answer in the back of the book

CHAPTER 3

Jehu's Arrow

Jehu was a commander in the army, under King Ahab and his son, King Joram. King Joram ruled the northern kingdom of Israel. His name "Joram" is also spelled "Jehoram" in which Joram is a shortened form of Jehoram. Jehu, the servant of King Joram, kills him with an arrow.

And Jehu drew a bow with his full strength,
and smote Jehoram between his arms,
and the arrow went out at his heart,
and he sunk down in his chariot.
2 Kings 9:24 KJV

Note of Interests: There are 2 kings in the Bible referred to as King Jehoram/Joram. The 1st King Jehoram was the son of King Jehoshaphat. He reigned in Judah, the southern kingdom from 853 to 841 BC. The son of Ahab is the other King Jehoram who reigned over the northern kingdom called Israel from 852 to 841 BC. They were brothers-in-law to each other. Jehoram, the son of Jehoshaphat, married

Athaliah, the daughter of King Ahab, the sister of King Joram/Jehoram of Israel.

Jehu, the son of Jehoshaphat, grandson of Nimshi, became the 10th king of the northern kingdom called Israel. He was raised to power by God for a specific purpose. God had Jehu anointed to overthrow the dynasty of Ahab and exterminate his heirs for the evil he had done. The history surrounding Jehu is found in 2 Kings, chapters 9 and 10.

Note of Interests: Elijah had prophesied the demise of Ahab's dynasty. He also foretold the manner in which King Ahab and Queen Jezebel would die because of the scandal of Naboth's vineyard resulting in his death, 1 Kings 21.

King Joram of Israel had been severely wounded in the battle at Ramoth-Gilead while defending it against the army of King Hazael of Aram. He went to Jezreel to recover, and King Ahaziah of Judah came to visit him. King Ahaziah was the son of Ahab and Jezebel; the king of the northern Kingdom of Israel, and he reigned from Samaria.

According to 2 Kings 9:1 – 4, Elisha the prophet summoned one of the young prophets to go to Ramoth-Gilead and find Jehu, the son of Jehoshaphat. Elisha told him to take Jehu to a private room away from his friends and pour on oil on his head and declare, what the Lord says, "I anoint you king over Israel. You are to strike down the house of your master

Ahab to avenge the blood of God's servants the prophets." Afterward, the young prophet was to open the door and run. The young prophet found Jehu sitting with the other army officers. He told Jehu he had a private message for him. The young prophet delivered the message and then opened the door and ran, 2 Kings 9:5 – 10.

When Jehu went back to his fellow officers, one of them asked him, is all well? And why did this madman visit him? First, Jehu tried to play it off. Then one of the men, told Jehu, he was hiding something, and for him to tell them. When Jehu told them what the young prophet said, they quickly took their garments off and put it under Jehu's bare steps. They blew the trumpet and proclaimed, "Jehu is king!" 2 Kings 9:11 – 13.

According to 2 Kings 9:15, after King Joram was wounded in battle, he returned to Jezreel to recover. Jehu told the men with him, "If you want me to be king, then don't let anyone escape this city because they will tell the news in Jezreel. Jezreel was about 54 miles from Ramoth-Gilead. Immediately, Jehu got in his chariot and rode to Jezreel where Joram was recuperating from battle.

Beginning at 2 Kings 9:17, the guard in the watchtower at Jezreel, shouted to the king, "I see a group of men coming this way." King Joram ordered the watchman to send a horseman out to ask them, "If they come in peace?" When the horseman arrived, he asked Jehu, "Have he come in peace?" Jehu told the horseman to get behind him with the rest of the troops." The watchman reported to the king that the horseman has reached them, but he is not coming back. The king sent out a 2ⁿᵈ horseman to asked, the same question, but the 2ⁿᵈ horseman did the same thing as the 1ˢᵗ horseman.

As the group of men came closer, the watchman shouted, "The leader of the group of men is driving his chariot like a madman, just like Jehu!" King Joram and Ahaziah set out in their chariots to meet Jehu on the plot of land that once belonged to Naboth the Jezreelite, 2 Kings 9:21.

King Joram asked Jehu, "Had he came in peace." Jehu replied, "How can there be peace as long as the idolatry of your mother Jezebel abounds?" King Joram turned his chariot around and fled, and shouted out to Ahaziah, "This is treachery, Ahaziah."

According to 2 Kings 9:24, Jehu drew his bow and shot King Joram between the shoulders. The arrow pierced his heart, he slumped down in his chariot and died.

Jehu commanded his assistant Bidkar, to throw his body in the field that Naboth once owned. Joram's body was thrown there, just as it was prophesied by Elijah.

When King Ahaziah saw what was happening, he fled. Jehu pursued him shouting, "Shoot him too!" So, they shot Ahaziah in his chariot as he fled to Megiddo where he died. King Ahaziah's servant carried him by chariot to Jerusalem and buried him in his ancestor's tomb.

Beginning at verse 30 of 2 Kings 9, Jehu headed to Jezreel to kill Queen Jezebel. When Jezebel heard he was coming she put on eyeshadow and brushed her hair. She then stood at the window, waiting for him to arrive. As Jehu walked through the city gate, she shouted down to him, "Why did you come here, you murderer? You're no better than Zimri, who murdered his master!"

Note of Interests: In the Bible, there are at least 2 Zimri. The son of Salu, a Simeonite prince, Number 25:14. Phinehas, the son of the priest Eleazar saw Zimri take a Midianite woman named Cozbi into his tent. He went into Zimri's tent with a javelin in his hand and thrust them both. The other Zimri was the 5th king of the northern kingdom of Israel. He killed King Elah, had his heirs murdered, and declared himself king. Zimri reigned for only 7 days because Omri, the commander of the army, stage an attacked against him. Zimri went into the palace, set it afire, and died in the flames, 1 Kings 16.

While Jezebel was standing in the window, Jehu looked up at the window and shouted, "Who is on my side?" A few eunuchs stuck their heads out of a window, and Jehu shouted, "Throw her out the window!" So, they did. Jezebel's blood splattered on the walls and the horses as they trampled upon her body.

Jehu told workers, "To make sure she has a proper burial because she was a king daughter." When they went out to bury her body, they could only find her skull, her hands, and feet. They told this to Jehu, and he said, "The Lord told Elijah that dogs would eat Jezebel's body, and her remains will be scattered over the ground like manure."

Note of Interests: Jehu executed Ahab's entire family. He also killed Ahab's friends, officials, and Baal's temple priests; then Jehu converted the pagan temple into a public toilet.

The Lord blessed Jehu for his obedience, and his dynasty lasted 4 generations. Jehu slowly started practicing idolatry, and God gradually gave Israel over to Hazael of Syria. Jehu reigned over Israel for 28 years, died of natural causes, and was succeeded by his son Jehoahaz, 2 Kings 10:30 – 36.

CHAPTER 4

Jehoash Shot an Arrow

The 5th place in the Bible where the word "arrow" is mentioned is 2nd Kings 13:17.

It reads:

"Open the east window," he said, and he opened it.
"Shoot!" Elisha said, and he shot.
"The Lord's arrow of victory, the
arrow of victory over Aram!"
Elisha declared.
"You will completely destroy the Arameans at Aphek."
2 Kings 13:17 NIV

The books of 1st and 2nd Kings were initially one book. They are the last two books of "Deuteronomistic History." The other Deuteronomistic History books are Joshua, Judges, 1st and 2nd Samuel.

The Deuteronomistic History is the history of Israel that explains the destruction of the Kingdom of Judah. It presents the history of ancient Israel and Judah from the death of King David to the release of Jehoiachin from

Babylon captivity; approximately 400 years from 960 – 560 BC.

The Book of Kings author is not mentioned, but Jewish tradition credits the prophet Jeremiah as the author of 1st and 2nd Kings, and many Bible scholars are divided on this. The Book of 2 Kings was written between 560 and 540 BC. The Book of 2 Kings has 25 chapters and can be outlined as follows.

1. Elijah and Elisha, 2 Kings 1 – 13
2. History of the Divided Kingdom, 2 Kings 14 – 17
3. History of the King Hezekiah of Judah, 2 Kings 18 – 20
4. History of the Southern Kingdom; Judah, 2 Kings 21 – 25

So, who was Jehoash during this era? He is also known as Joash, and his name means "Given by The Lord." He was the son of King Ahaziah and Zibiah, a woman of Beersheba, 2 Kings 12:1. Jehoash was the 9th king of Judah. He began to reign when he was 7 years old and reigned 40 years.

While Jehoash was an infant, his life was saved by his aunt, Jehosheba. She was the daughter of King Jehoram/Joram who was the husband of Athaliah. Jehosheba was also the sister of King Ahaziah, and the wife of Jehoiada, the high priest. She hid Jehoash and his nurse from the massacre of his family. He became the sole surviving son of King Ahaziah, after the slaughter of the royal family that was ordered by his grandmother, Athaliah.

Athaliah was considered the daughter of King Ahab and Queen Jezebel, the ruler of the northern kingdom of Israel. She was given in marriage at an early age to King Jehoram/Joram of the southern kingdom of Judah. The marriage sealed a treaty between the two kingdoms. Her son, Ahaziah reigned for 1 year and was killed by Jehu at the age of 23. She became queen by seizing the throne of Judah. She ordered the execution of all possible heirs to the throne. Queen Athaliah established the worship of Baal in Judah and reigned for 6 years.

Jehoash's uncle, the high priest, named Jehoiada brought him forth to the people when he was 7 years old. He was crowned and anointed king of Judah. Queen Athaliah was taken by surprise when she heard the shout of the people, "Long live the king." When she appeared, Jehoiada the priest commanded that she be led out of the temple and put to death, along with anyone that tries to rescue her, 2 Kings 11:13 – 20.

Jehoash reigned in Jerusalem for 40 years. While the High Priest Jehoiada lived, King Jehoash worshipped God and observed His laws, 2 Kings 12:2. After Jehoiada death, Jehoash fell into evil practices, and the land was defiled with the worship of idols.

According to 2 Kings 13:14 – 20, Elisha became sick, and King Jehoash of Israel went to visit him. Elisha told Jehoash, "Take a bow and some arrows," and Jehoash did as he was told. Then Elisha said to the king, "Put your hand on the bow," and Jehoash put his hand on the bow. Then Elisha laid his hands over the king's hands and told him to "Open the east window." Jehoash opened the window, then Elisha said, "Shoot." Jehoash shot, then Elisha said, "This is the Lord's arrow of victory over Aram, and you will defeat them at Aphek!"

Next, Elisha told the king to "Take the arrows!" Jehoash took the arrows and then Elisha said to him "Strike the ground!" Jehoash strikes the ground 3 times and stopped. Elisha told Jehoash, "He should have strike the ground 5 or 6 times, then he would have defeated Aram until he annihilated them!" Elisha told King Jehoash, "He will be victorious over the Aram only 3 times," 2 Kings 13:18 – 19.

Note of Interests: Aram was one of the sons of Shem, and Shem was one of the sons of Noah, Genesis 10:22. Ancient Aram is a region frequently mentioned in the Bible which is present-day Syria. The Arameans are Syrians. Some Bible translations such as CEV, ESV, and KJV when translating the Hebrew word for "Aramean," substitute the word "Syrian" instead. The NIV, NLT, NASB are Bible translations that use the word "Aramean" in scripture.

According to the last 6 verses of 2 Kings 13, Elisha died and was buried in a tomb. Some Israelites were burying a man when they saw a band of raiders, and they quickly threw the corpse in the tomb of Elisha and fled. When the dead man body touched Elisha's bones, he came to life and stood on his feet.

Meanwhile, King Hazael of Aram oppressed Israel throughout the reign of Jehoahaz. The Lord had mercy on Israel because of his covenant with Abraham, Isaac, and Jacob. And to this day, the Lord has been unwilling to destroy them from His presence, 2 Kings 13:23.

When King Hazael died, his son Ben-Hadad became king. Jehoash, the son of King Jehoahaz, took back from Ben-Hadad the cities that Hazael had taken in battle from his father. King Jehoash defeated Ben-Hadad 3 times and recovered Israel's cities and towns, 2 Kings 13:24 – 25.

CHAPTER 5

Nor Shoot an Arrow

Hezekiah was the 13th king of Judah, and he trusted in the Lord, the God of Israel. His name means "Jehovah Strengthens" in Hebrew. He was the son of Ahaz the king of Judah and his mother was Abijah. Abijah was the daughter of Zechariah, the high priest. Hezekiah began to reign when he was 25 years old, and he reigned in Jerusalem for 29 years, 2 Kings 18:2.

King Hezekiah was one of the most noticeable kings of Judah. He did what was right in the eyes of the Lord. King Hezekiah kept the commandments the Lord gave Moses. He destroyed high places, sacred stones, cut down Asherah poles, and broke into pieces the bronze snake where the Israelites had burned incense.

King Hezekiah purified the Temple, purged the idols and reformed the priesthood. The Passover Feast recommenced under his reign. He was successful in whatever he set out to do, 2 Kings 18:6 – 7. Hezekiah died of natural causes at the age of 54, and he was succeeded by his son Manasseh, 2 Kings 20:21.

Note of Interests: In the Gospel of Matthew, Hezekiah is mentioned in the genealogy of Jesus, Matthew 1:9 and 10. The history of Hezekiah's reign is recorded in 2 Kings, chapters 18 – 20; Isaiah, chapters 36 – 39; and 2 Chronicles, chapters 29 – 32. He reigns between 715 and 686 BC. King Hezekiah is also mentioned in the books of the prophets: Isaiah, Jeremiah, Hosea, and Micah. The Book of Proverbs was "copied by the officials of King Hezekiah of Judah" which is a collection of King Solomon's proverbs, Proverbs 25:1.

The biblical event in Israel's history that led up to the words "Nor Shoot an Arrow" is as follow.

**Therefore, thus said the Lord
concerning the king of Assyria,
He shall not come into this city,
nor shoot an arrow there,
nor come before it with shield,
nor cast a bank against it.**
2 Kings 19:32 KJV

In the 4th year of King Hezekiah's reign, king of Assyria marched against Samaria and captured it in 3 years. According to 2 Kings 18:12, this happened because Samaria had continually disobeyed the Lord their God commandments. In the 14th year of King Hezekiah's reign,

Sennacherib king of Assyria attacked all the fortified cities of Judah and captured them.

So, Hezekiah king of Judah sent a message to Sennacherib, the king of Assyria. The message stated, "he was guilty of rebellion, and if he withdrew from Judah, he would pay him whatever he demanded." The king of Assyria took from Hezekiah 300 talents of silver and 30 talents of gold. He was given all the silver that was found in the temple of the Lord. The gold that covered the doors and doorposts of the temple was also given to the king of Assyria, 2 Kings 18:14 – 16.

Beginning at 2 Kings 18:17, Sennacherib sent his supreme commander, his chief officer, and his field commander with an army from Lachish to King Hezekiah at Jerusalem. They called out for King Hezekiah, and Eliakim the palace administrator, Shebna the scribe, and Joah the recorder went out to them.

King Sennacherib's field commander said, "Come now, make a bargain with his master, the king of Assyria," 2 Kings 18:23. The people on the wall was told by Sennacherib's field commander, not to let King Hezekiah deceive them, King Hezekiah cannot deliver them from Assyria's hands, don't be persuaded to trust in the Lord when King Hezekiah says, the Lord will deliver them, and the city from the king of Assyria, 2 Kings 18:30.

The people remained silent and said nothing, 2 Kings 18:36. Then Eliakim, Shebna, Joah went to Hezekiah with their clothes torn and relayed the words of Assyria' field commander. According to 2 Kings 19, after King Hezekiah heard the message, he tore his clothes, put on sackcloth, and went into the temple of the Lord. He sent Eliakim, Shebna and the leading priest, all wearing sackcloth to the prophet Isaiah, son of Amoz to tell him what the Assyrian commander had said.

When King Hezekiah's officials came to Isaiah, Isaiah told them to tell Hezekiah that the Lord said, "Do not be afraid of the words he had heard from the king of Assyria who has blasphemed Him." The Lord said, "The king of Assyria will return to his own country, and there he will be killed by his own sword in his own land," 2 King 19:7.

Sennacherib sent another message to the people of Jerusalem. It said, "Do not let the god King Hezekiah depend on, deceive you. You have heard what Assyria's kings have done to all the countries; destroyed them completely," 2 Kings 19:9 – 13.

Hezekiah went up to the temple and prayed to the Lord after he received the letter from the messengers, 2 Kings 19:14. He acknowledged that He is God over all the kingdoms of the earth, who have made heaven and earth. He admitted that the Assyrian kings have laid waste to many nations, their lands, and thrown their gods into the fire. Hezekiah then asked the Lord their God to deliver them from the Assyrian kings' hand, so that all the kingdoms of the earth will know that He alone, is Lord, 2 Kings 19:19.

Isaiah, the son of Amoz, sent another message to Hezekiah. "The Lord, the God of Israel, have heard your prayer concerning Sennacherib, king of Assyria." In the message, the Lord says the king of Assyria will not enter Jerusalem or shoot an arrow there, 2 Kings 19:32. The king of Assyria will not come before it with a shield or build a siege ramp against it. King Sennacherib will return the way he came, and he will not enter this city, declares the Lord. The Lord will defend the city for his sake, and for the sake of David, his servant, 2 Kings 19:34.

According to 2 Kings 19:35, the same night the angel of the Lord put to death 185,000 men in the Assyrian camp. When the people got up the next morning, there were dead bodies, everywhere. Sennacherib, the king of Assyria broke camp and withdrew, and returned to Nineveh.

One day, Sennacherib was worshiping in the temple of his god Nisrock, and his sons Adrammelek and Sharezer killed him with the sword. Afterward, they escaped to the land of Ararat, and Esarhaddon, his son, succeeded him as king.

CHAPTER 6

No Arrow Can Make Him Flee

The Book of Job is the 18th book in the King James Bible. It is considered the strangest book in the Hebrew Bible. The Book of Job author is unknown. However, Moses the lawgiver, Solomon the wisest man who ever lived, and even suffering Job have been considered the author.

The Book of Job is also hard to pinpoint the date it was written. Some scholars believe it was written between 2100 – 1800 BC. According to other biblical scholars, the Book of Job was written a few centuries after the flood of Noah between 1656 and 2348 BC. Eliphaz, one of Job friend, refers to the flood as being in the past, Job 22:16.

Other scholars believe some of the first 5 books of Moses were written after the time of the Patriarchs, and this place the Book of Job around 1500 BC. Therefore, the Book of Job is believed to be the oldest book in the Bible by some scholars.

Some of the other reasons why the Book of Job is believed to be the oldest book in the Bible by some scholars are listed below.

1. Job sacrifices to God as the head of his family; this was a practice during the patriarchal age that stopped with Moses, Job 1:5.
2. Job's daughters were granted an inheritance along with his sons, a patriarchal tradition that also ended with Moses, Job 42:15.
3. Kesitah was a piece of money mentioned in the Book of Job which belongs to the patriarchal age, Job 42:11, OJB (Orthodox Jewish Bible).

Note of Interests: The patriarchal age is the era of 3 biblical patriarchs who were Abraham, Isaac, and Jacob according to Genesis 12 – 50. This era tells of man's earliest relationship with God. Scholars place this era between 1950 and 1500 BC. The word "patriarch" means "father-ruler."

The first poetic book in the Old Testament is the Book of Job, and it has 42 chapters. The only individuals mentioned in the Book of Job are Job, his wife who is not named, Eliphaz, Bildad, Zophar, and Elihu.

Question: What are the other poetic books of the Old Testament? *smile*

Answer in the back of the book.

The name "Job" name means "persecuted." Job was a wealthy individual living in a land called Uz. He had a wife with 7 sons and 3 daughters. He owned 7,000 sheep, 3,000 camels, 500 pairs of oxen, 500 donkeys, and many servants. Job was considered the most righteous and wealthiest man in the East.

Job was blameless and upright, always careful to avoid doing evil. He was a righteous and upright man whom God allowed to be tested by Satan. Job endured many tragedies and hardship but remains faithful to God.

There was a man in the land of Uz,
Whose name was Job; and that man
was perfect and upright,
and one that feared God, and eschewed evil.
Job 1:1 KJV

The Book of Job has 42 chapters which can be outlined as follow.

Chapters 1 - 3
In the 1ˢᵗ chapter of Job, God and Satan are discussing a man name "Job." God allows Job's faithfulness to be tested by Satan. God told Satan, "Behold, all that he has is in your power, only do not put forth your hand on him."

In brief, Satan appears before God in heaven. God boasts to Satan about Job's goodness, but Satan argues that Job is only good because God has blessed him abundantly. Satan challenges God that, if permitted to punish Job, he will turn and curse Him, Job 1:1 – 11. God allows Satan to torment Job, but God forbids Satan to take Job's life in the process.

In the course of one day, Job receives 4 messages each containing devastating news. A gang of Sabeans attacked and stole the oxen and donkeys, and his servants were killed. While that servant was still speaking another servant ran up saying that God sent down fire from heaven that killed his sheep and servants. Before he finished speaking a third servant raced to Job and said, "Three gangs of Chaldeans attacked and stole his camels." While he was speaking a fourth servant rushed up and said, "Your children were having a feast at the home of his oldest son, suddenly a windstorm blew down the house and killed all his children," Job 1:13 – 19. Job tears his clothes from his body, shaves his head and mourn, but he still blessed God in his prayers, Job 1:20.

Satan appears before God again, and God grants him another chance to test Job faithfulness. This time Satan afflicted Job with painful skin sores. His wife encourages Job to curse God and die. Job refuses to curse God even in his dire condition, Job 2:1 – 10.

Three of Job's friends, Eliphaz the Temanite from Teman, Bildad the Shuhite from Shuah, and Zophar the Naamathite from Naamah came to visit him. They sit with Job in silence for 7 days and nights out of respect for his mourning, Job 2:1 – 13.

Job's 1st speech begins in chapter 3 where he curses the day he was born, wishes that he had died at birth, and long for death.

Chapters 4 – 37

Beginning in chapter 4, Job begins a conversation with his 4 friends. They share their thoughts on Job's afflictions in long, poetic statements. Job's friends give him plenty of bad advice, makes wrong assumptions, and spoke harsh words to him in several rounds of discussion which are recorded in chapters 5 – 37 of Job.

Job's friends mistakenly blamed Job sufferings on his sins and his children's sins rather than God testing Job. Job responds to each of his friend remarks throughout these chapters. Job grows irritated of his friends and calls them "worthless physicians," Job 13:4.

Chapter 38 – 42

God speaks to Job and humbles him by asking a series of questions that could only be answered by God. Beginning in chapter 38, God asked Job, where was he when He laid the foundation of the earth, did he ever tell the sun to rise, has he ever walked on the ocean floor, can he arrange stars in groups? In chapter 39, God asked Job, does he know when the mountain goats give birth, who gave horses their strength, did he teach the hawks to fly south for the winter? In chapter 40, God continues to talk to Job. In chapter 41, God asked Job can he catch a sea monster?

In chapter 41 of Job is where the words "no arrow can make him flee," verse 28. This phrase is referring to a giant sea creature called a "Leviathan" in the Bible. Some scholars believe it is referring to a crocodile, dragon or a serpent; the exact identity is unknown.

The arrow cannot make him flee (Leviathan):
slingstones are turned with him into stubble.
Job 41:28 KJV

God speaks about and describes the Leviathan in the entire chapter of Job 41 with 32 verses. God uses the defines of the Leviathan to make known to Job just how powerless he is against this creature. If he cannot go head to head with a Leviathan how could he ever hope to stand against the God who made and masters Leviathan?

In the end, Job answers God by saying, "I have declared that which I did not understand," Job 42:3. So God blessed the latter part of Job's life more than the first. He returns Job's health, providing him with twice as much property as before (14,000 sheep, 6,000 camels, 1,000 yokes of oxen, and 1,000 donkeys), another set of children (7 sons and 3 daughters), and long life (Job lived to be 140 years old, and saw 4 generations), Job 42:12 – 17.

CHAPTER 7

Make Ready Their Arrow

The word "Psalms" is derived from the Greek word "psalmoi" meaning "instrumental music." The Book of Psalms is a collection of poems, short stories, plays, songs, and excerpts by several authors. It is the 2nd poetic book of the Bible in the Old Testament.

The Book of Psalms has 150 chapters, the most chapters than the other books of the Bible but not words. The longest chapter in Psalms is 119 with 176 verses, KJV. Psalm 119 is an acrostic Psalm. It has 22 sections with 8 lines, and each line in each section starts with a Hebrew letter in the alphabet. Psalm 119 is the longest Psalm as well as the longest chapter in the Bible, 1st verse reads as follow.

Blessed are the undefiled in the way,
who walk in the law of the Lord.
Psalms 119:1 KJV

The shortest chapter in the Book of Psalms is Psalm 117 with 2 verses. It's one of the 5 Hallel Psalms that is sung as part of the Passover service. The Hallel Psalms are Psalms

113 – 118. Jesus sang these Psalms with His disciples, Matthew 26:30, Mark 14:26. Psalm 117 reads as follow.

1. O praise the Lord, all ye nations:
praise him, all ye people.
2. For his merciful kindness is great toward us:
and the truth of the Lord endureth for ever.
Praise ye the Lord.
Psalm 117:1 – 2 KJV

Most of Psalms are linked to David's life and life experiences. King David did not write all of Psalms, but he is credited with 80 Psalms out of 150. The other authors are Asaph, Moses, Solomon, the sons of Korah, Ethan the Ezrahite, and Heman the Ezrahite.

Note of Interests: Asaph is the author of Psalms 50 and 73 – 83. He was one of David's 3 chief musicians, and Heman and Ethan are the other 2. Ethan is the author of Psalm 89, and Heman is the author of Psalm 88. The Sons of Korah were the sons of Moses' cousin, Korah. Korah led a revolt against Moses, and God sent fire from heaven and killed him and consume 249 of his followers, but the children of Korah were not killed, Numbers 26:11. They wrote Psalms 42 – 50, 62, and 72 – 85.

The Book of Psalms is divided into 5 sections with each closing with a benediction; a short "prayer of praise." The 5 divisions do not have a specific title, but scholars believe the division mirror the 5 books of the Torah; Genesis, Exodus,

Leviticus, Numbers and Deuteronomy were written by Moses. They are listed below with their short benedictions.

1. Section 1   Psalms 1 – 41
    Blessed be the Lord God of Israel from everlasting, and to everlasting. Amen and Amen. (Psalm 41:13 KJV)
2. Section 2   Psalms 42 – 72
    And blessed be his glorious name for ever: and let the whole earth be filled with his glory; Amen, and Amen. (Psalm 72:19 KJV)
3. Section 3   Psalms 73 – 89
    Blessed be the Lord for evermore. Amen, and Amen. (Psalm 89:52 KJV)
4. Section 4   Psalms 90 – 106
    Blessed be the Lord God of Israel from everlasting to everlasting: and let all the people say, Amen. Praise ye the Lord. (Psalm 106:48 KJV)
5. Section 5   Psalms 107 – 150
    Let every thing that hath breath praise the Lord. Praise ye the Lord. (Psalm 150:6 KJV)

Note of Interests: The Book of Psalms is quoted around 75 times in the New Testament. Jesus quoted from the Book of Psalms more than any other book of the Bible. He quoted from the Book of Exodus 7 times, Isaiah 8 times, Deuteronomy 10 times, and Psalms on 11 occasions. The Book of Romans written by Paul refers to Psalms about 14 times. The Book of Psalms is the most-read book of the Bible.

The 11th chapter of Psalms has only 7 verses. In this chapter, David encourages himself in God against his enemies. Psalm 11 is believed to be written when David began to feel the resentment of Saul's envy. David was in the court of Saul when Saul threw a javelin at David for the second time trying to kill him. David is encouraged to flee. This Psalm is written about the dangerous situations the righteous faces under the hand the wicked.

Beginning in verse 1 of Psalm 11, David is saying to his friends, "In the Lord, he will take refuge. Don't say to him to escape like a bird to the mountains!" David's friends want him to run from King Saul because he is bent on David demise.

In verse 2 of Psalm 11 is where the word "arrow" is mentioned. David said,

"For, lo, the wicked bend their bow,
they make ready their arrow upon the string,
that they may privily shoot at the upright in heart."
Psalm 11:2 KJV

In brief:
Beginning in chapter 17 of 1 Samuel, the Philistines and the Israelites armies were camped on opposite hills with a valley between them. The Philistines' giant named Goliath was over 9 feet tall, and for 40 days, he shouted out to the army of Israel to choose their best warrior to come out and fight him. If he won, the Israelites would become the Philistines slaves. If he didn't win, the Philistines would become Israel slaves. King Saul and his men were terrified.

One day, Jesse told David to take his brothers a sack of roasted grain and 10 loaves of bread to the army's camp. David heard the threats of Goliath and decided to take the challenge of Goliath. After David killed Goliath, from that point forward King Saul kept David in his service. Whatever King Saul asked David to do, he did it successfully. Soon Saul made him a commander over the men of war, and they were victorious in battles. King Saul begins to envy David because the people loved him. King Saul feared for his kingdom and tried to kill David, on several occasions.

In Psalm 11, David's friends tell him to flee from Saul. In verses 1 – 3, David asks his friends why they are telling him to flee. His friends answer, "The godless want to kill the righteous."

In Psalm 11:4 – 6, David believes the Lord is in the temple, and the Lord sees the righteous and the wicked people. David explains that God will punish them and gave 3 descriptive punishments which are listed below.

1. Fiery Coal that Burns
2. Burning Sulfur
3. Scorching Wind

Psalm 11 ends with a beautiful and wonderful promise.
For the Lord is righteous, he loves justice;
the upright will see his face.
Psalm 11:7 NIV

CHAPTER 8

God Shall Shoot

David is the author of Psalm 64, and this Psalm is titled, "To the Chief Musician; A Psalm of David." The phrase, "To the Chief Musician; A Psalm of David" occurs at the beginning of 18 Psalms; NKJV.

In verse 7 of Psalm 64 is where these words "God shall shoot" are written by David.

> **But God shall shoot at them with an arrow;**
> **suddenly shall they be wounded.**
> Psalm 64:7 KJV

David would write psalms and deliver them to the chief musician of the temple to use in worship. The chief musician was the head director of the sacred music of the sanctuary.

Psalm 64 is about David's enemies, persecutors, slanderers and the trouble they created for him. David prays to God to preserve him from his enemies' evil plots. He cries out to God concerning his crisis, but the crisis that's connected to this specific Psalm is unknown.

personal and up-close. They are
\ from his life experiences. Scholars
author of 80 Psalms out of 150. The
wny David wrote a Psalm is given for 13 of them,
and they are listed below.

The Book of Psalms is divided into 5 sections.

Section 1   Psalms 1 - 41
1. Psalm 3 – A Psalm of David when he fled from his son Absalom; 8 verses.
2. Psalm 7 – A Psalm of David when he sang to the Lord concerning the words of Cush, a Benjamite; 17 verses.
3. Psalm 18 – A Psalm of David when the Lord delivered him from the hand of all his enemies, including King Saul; 50 verses.
4. Psalm 34 – A Psalm of David when he pretended to be crazy before Abimelech, who drove him away and he departed; 22 verses.

Section 2   Psalm 42 - 72
1. Psalm 51 – A Psalm of David when Nathan the prophet went to David after he had slept with Bathsheba, the wife of Uriah the Hittite; 18 verses.
2. Psalm 52 – A Psalm of David when Doeg the Edomite went and told Saul, David has gone to the house of Ahimelech; 9 verses.
3. Psalm 54 – A Psalm of David when the Ziphites told Saul, David wasn't hiding with them; 7 verses.
4. Psalm 56 – A Psalm of David when the Philistines captured him in Gath; 13 verses.

5. Psalm 57 – A Psalm of David when he fled t. Saul in a cave; 11 verses.
6. Psalm 59 – A Psalm of David when Saul sent men to watch his house in order to kill him; 17 verses.
7. Psalm 60 – A Psalm of David when he fought against Mesopotamia and Syria of Zobah, and Joab his commander returned and killed 12,000 Edomites in the Valley of Salt; 12 verses.
8. Psalm 63 – A Psalm of David when he was in the wilderness of Judah; 11 verses.

Section 3 of Psalms consisted of chapters 73 – 89, and section 4 of Psalms consist of chapters 90 – 106. They contain a few Psalms of David but doesn't have an explanation for them.

Section 5   Psalms 107 – 150

1. Psalm 142 – A Psalm of David when he was in the cave; 7 verses.

The word "arrow" is mentioned in Psalm 64. It was written by David, but he gave no specific reason for this Psalm. The 10 verses in this chapter can be outlined as follow.

David Cries Out to God against the Wicked, verses 1 – 4

David prays to God to protect him from the wicked. They have secretly plotted against him, and they desire to do evil to him. The wicked words cut like a sword, and they aim cruel and bitter words at him that sting like a sharp arrow. They suddenly ambush and shoot innocent people.

The Secret Plotting of the Evil Doers, verses 5 – 6

The evil doers are determined to do evil to David. They encourage one another to set traps, and then say, "No one will see them." They make evil plans and think they can commit the perfect crime because no one knows their thoughts.

God Hears and Answers David Cries, verses 7 – 9

God shall shoot at David's enemies with an arrow, and they will be wounded. Their tongues will be destroyed, and those who see this will flee. All the people will fear God, proclaim His mighty acts, and keep in mind what He has done.

The Decision of the Righteous, verse 10

The righteous will rejoice in the Lord. They will declare His works and take refuge in Him. God's answer to David's prayer demonstrates God only needed one arrow, vs. 7; while the enemies shot "arrows" of bitter words at David, vs. 3. God is trustworthy, faithful and worthy to be praised.

Note of Interests: The word "arrows" is mentioned in verses 3, while the word "arrow" without the "s" is mentioned in verse 7. The word "arrows" is mentioned in 39 verses in the King James Bible, and twice in the same verse of 1 Samuel 20:21, and 2 Kings 13:15. The word "arrows" is mentioned in 15 books of the Bible. It is mentioned the most in the book of Psalms, a total of 13 times. Listed below is where the word "arrows" with the "s" is mentioned.

Numbers 24:8	Deuteronomy 32:23	Deuteronomy 32:42
1 Samuel 20:20	**1 Samuel 20:21***	**1 Samuel 20:22**
1 Samuel 20:36	**1 Samuel 20:38**	2 Samuel 22:15

2 Kings 13:15*	2 Kings 13:18	1 Chronicles 12:2
2 Chronicles 26:15	Job 6:4	Psalm 7:13
Psalm 18:14	Psalm 21:12	Psalm 38:2
Psalm 45:5	Psalm 57:4	Psalm 58:7
Psalm 64:3	Psalm 76:3	Psalm 77:17
Psalm 120:4	Psalm 127:4	Psalm 144:6
Proverbs 26:18	Isaiah 5:28	Isaiah 7:24
Jeremiah 50:9	**Jeremiah 50:14**	Jeremiah 51:11
Lamentations 3:13	Ezekiel 5:16	Ezekiel 21:21
Ezekiel 39:3	Ezekiel 39:9	Habakkuk 3:11

Glory Be To God! As I was looking over this section, the unction of the Holy Spirit stirred in my spirit; Shamatastata, Hallelujah. I truly believe that Father God is asking you, the reader, to read each of the above chapters surrounding "arrows;" one chapter per day in KJV, NIV and NLT versions, each day, until you have finished reading them all, and that would be 31 days. Be Bless in Jesus' Name. Amen. (12/15/18 @0838, I'm starting now)

Your Starting Date: _____ smile . . .

CHAPTER 9

Arrow that Flies

Psalm 91 has 16 verses. This Psalm has no title, nor is the writer of this psalm is mentioned. Jewish traditions states, when the author's name is not mentioned in a psalm, the last named mentioned in the previous Psalm or Psalms is the writer of that Psalm, also. Therefore, this would be considered another Psalm of Moses. In Psalm 91 there are many similar expressions like those by Moses, in the Book of Deuteronomy. There are other scholars that credit Psalm 91 to David.

The Midrash believes that Moses wrote Psalm 91 on the day he completed the building of the Tabernacle in the wilderness. These verses describe how Moses felt when he entered the Tabernacle, being engulfed in a divine cloud.

The Tabernacle was a portable tent sanctuary in the wilderness for the Israelites. God ordered them to build it after they were freed from the Egyptian captivity while wandering in the wilderness. The Tabernacle is the sanctuary where God dwelt among his people, Exodus 25:8.

Note of Interests: Midrash was a group of ancient Jewish commentaries and interpreters. They translated Hebrew's Scriptures to obtain a principle of Jewish law and layout a moral belief. The word "Midrash" means "to seek out" or "to investigate."

Jewish people believe reciting Psalm 91 will protection and rescue them from danger. Psalm 91 refers to several types of evil that threaten a man which are "Terror," "Arrow," "Pestilence," and "Destruction" mentioned in verses 5 – 6. The Talmud calls this Psalm the "song of plagues," for he who recites it with faith in God believing He will be helped by God in time of danger. During the era of the Geonim, Psalm 91 was recited to drive away demons and evil spirits.

Note of Interests: Geonim is a period that lasted from the 7th century until the 11th century, approximately 400 years. This period is named after the Geonim. They were the heads of the rabbinic academies in Babylonia. They had a prominent and decisive role in the teaching of the Torah and Jewish Law.

The 91st Psalm is used during Lent. Lent is 40 days before Easter observed by Christians, not counting Sundays. It's a period of fasting, repentance, self-control, self-denial, and spiritual discipline. It's a time to reflect on Jesus Christ, his suffering, his sacrifice, his life, death, burial, and resurrection. Lent begins on Ash Wednesday and ends before Easter Sunday.

The 91st Psalm is a regular ritual of Jewish, Catholic, Anglican and Protestant public worship. This psalm has been set to music and paraphrased in hymns. A person finds strength when trouble arises in the knowledge that God is there protecting and caring for you. Psalm 91 gives you the confidence to trust in God.

The 91st Psalm is read as a prayer for protection. It is often said before an individual embarking on a journey. Psalm 91 is repeated aloud 7 times during a burial ceremony. The 11th verse of Psalm 91 is recited after "Shalom Aleichem" which means "peace be upon you." Shalom Aleichem is a traditional Jewish song sung every Friday night upon your return home from the synagogue prayer. It welcomes the angels who accompany a person home on the eve of the Sabbath.

For he will command his angels
concerning you to guard you in all your ways.
Psalm 91:11 NIV

The devil quoted from Psalm 91, verses 11 and 12 during the temptation of Jesus in the wilderness, Matthew 4:6 and Luke 4:10 – 11.

For he will order his angels to
protect you wherever you go.
They will hold you up with their hands

so you won't even hurt your foot on a stone.
Psalm 91:11 – 12 NLT

Note of Interests: Psalm 91 is known as the Soldier's Psalm.

--------------◆◇◆--------------

Psalm 91 expresses, whosoever chooses God for his protector shall find all in him that he needs. He is protected from the snares of the fowler which is the temptations of Satan, and from the noisome pestilence of sin. There is comfort, contentment, peace, safety, and security to the believers in the midst of danger. They shall see God's promises fulfilled and observe the downfall of their enemies.

God will in due time deliver them out of trouble, and always be with them in trouble.

The 16 verses of Psalm 91 can be outlined as follow:
1. He Who Dwells in the Secret Place of the Most-High, verses 1 – 2
    Find Shelter in God's Presence
    Can Trust God
2. Safety from the Most-High, verses 3 – 8
    He Will Deliver You
    He Will Cover You
    You Will Not Fear
    You Will Only Observe
3. The Servants of the Most-High, verses 9 – 13
    Receive Promises
    Receive Protection
    Receive Provision
    Receive Power

4. The Promises from the Most-High, verses 14 – 16
   He Will Deliver Him
   He Will Protect Him
   He Will Answer Him
   He Will Be with Him in Trouble
   He Will Honor Him
   He Will Satisfy Him with Long Life
   He Will Show Him His Salvation

The word "arrow" is found in the 5ᵗʰ verse of Psalm 91, and verse 6 is a continuation of this verse. It reads as follow.

**5. You will not fear the terror of night,
nor the arrow that flies by day.
6. Nor the pestilence that stalks in the darkness,
nor the plague that destroys at midday.**
Psalm 91:5 – 6 NIV

CHAPTER 10

A Sharp Arrow

**A man that beareth false witness
against his neighbour is
a maul, and a sword, and a sharp arrow.**
Proverbs 25:18 KJV

The word "proverb" means "to be like." The Book of Proverbs is a collection of comparisons based on observations, serious thinking, remembering past behaviors, and experiences. The Book of Proverbs contains essays, poems, and sayings of ancient Israel. Scholars believe some of the material in Proverbs originated as folk wisdom, circulating in the tribes. The Book of Proverbs compares ordinary, everyday things and images to life's truths. Proverbs consist of moral and straightforward statements and teach fundamental realities about life.

The Book of Proverbs provides profound insights and uplifting wisdom on how to live a happy, honest, peaceful, and righteous life. Proverbs seek to enlighten individuals on how to conform to honest behavior, right thinking, and instruct them to live a moral life. It emphasizes that God is all-good and all-powerful, and He should be honored and respected.

King Solomon, the son of King David and Bathsheba, is credited as the primary author. Other contributors to Proverbs include a group of men called The Wise, Agur, and King Lemuel. Scholars believe Proverbs were written during the reign of Solomon, 971 – 931 BC.

The Book of Proverbs is one of the Poetic Books of the Bible. The other Poetic Books are Job, Psalms, Ecclesiastes, and the Song of Songs. These books contain advise, poetry, and wisdom. The Book of Job is the 1st Poetic Book. It makes known the sovereignty of God, and suffering is not a result of sin.

The Book of Psalms describes man everyday problems and his relationship with God. In the Book of Ecclesiastes is where you find God's wisdom that will keep you from ruining your life. It teaches that real success is in a relationship with God. Song of Songs which is also called Song of Solomon is a book to learn about relationships, and what couples should strive for in marriage.

The Book of Proverbs has 31 chapters. It teaches wisdom to the young, as well as the old, inexperienced and the learned. The Book of Proverbs can be outlined as follow.
1. The Virtues of Wisdom, Chapters 1 – 9
2. The Proverbs of Solomon, Chapter 10 – 22:16
3. The Sayings of the Wise, Chapter 22:17 – 24
4. More Proverbs of Solomon, Chapter 25 – 29

5. The Words of Agur, Chapter 30
6. The Words of King Lemuel, Chapter 31

The main subject in the Book of Proverbs is "The Fear of the Lord" which is found 14 times in 31 chapters; (Proverbs 1:7, 1:29, 2:5, 8:13, 9:10, 10:27, 14:26, 14:27, 15:16, 15:33, 16:6, 19:23, 22:4 and 23:17). The phrase "The Fear of the Lord" is only mentioned 27 times in the Bible; 26 in the Old Testament and once in the New Testament; Acts 9:31.

Then the church throughout Judea,
Galilee and Samaria
enjoyed a time of peace and was strengthened.
Living in the fear of the Lord and
encouraged by the Holy Spirit,
it increased in numbers.
Acts 9:31 NIV

A Few of My Parents Most Quoted Proverbs.

Proverbs 1:7   The fear of the Lord is the beginning of knowledge: but fools despise wisdom and instruction. KJV

Proverbs 3:5-6   Trust in the Lord with all thine heart; and lean not unto thine own understanding. In all your ways acknowledge him, and he shall direct thy paths. KJV

Proverbs 14:34   Righteousness exalteth a nation, but sin is a reproach to any people. KJV

Proverbs 22:1   A good name is rather to be chosen than great riches, and loving favour rather than silver and gold. KJV

Proverbs 22:6   Train up a child in the way he should go: and when he is old, he will not depart from it. KJV

Proverbs 22:15   Foolishness is bound in the heart of a child, but the rod of correction shall drive it far from him. KJV

Question: Out of the 6 Proverbs, there is only one my mom quoted, all the time, especially, in the time of hardships, worries, and difficulties. I can hear her soft, speaking voice, now. Which one do you believe is the Proverb? Praise God!

Answer in the back of book.

Three of My Favorite Proverbs:

Proverbs 16:18   A cheerful heart is good medicine, but a crushed spirit dries up the bones. NIV

Proverbs 21:1   In the Lord's hand the king's heart is a stream of water that he channels toward all who please him. NIV

Proverbs 27:17   As iron sharpens iron, so one person sharpens another. NIV

Now, What's Your Favorite Proverbs? *smile*

1. _____
2. _____
3. _____
4. _____
5. _____
6. _____

In the 25th chapter of Proverbs is where the word "arrow" is mentioned. This chapter has 28 verses and is titled "More Proverbs of Solomon," compiled by the men of Hezekiah.

These are more proverbs of Solomon,
collected by the advisers of King Hezekiah of Judah.
Proverbs 25:1 NLT

The 18 verse in Proverbs 25 is where the words "a sharp arrow" is mentioned. It reads.

Telling lies about others is as harmful
as hitting them with an ax,
wounding them with a sword or
shooting them with a sharp arrow.
Proverbs 25:18 NLT

Solomon is comparing telling lies on others as harmful as 3 things:

1. Hitting them with an ax
2. Wounding them with a sword
3. Shooting them with a sharp arrow

CHAPTER 11

Repetition

Isaiah 37 is a repetition of the biblical event in 2ⁿᵈ Kings 19. There are several biblical events, stories, and even whole books in which the Bible repeats. The use of repetition in the Bible emphasizes the importance of a person, theme, or event. The 10 Commandments are given in Exodus 20 and repeated in Deuteronomy 5. Repetition offers greater credibility, like the 4 Gospels. Also, repetition allows the writer to approach the biblical event from a different aspect or perspective, like the Book of Kings and the Books of Chronicles.

An outline of 2 Kings 19 and Isaiah 37 chapters are given below. The word "arrow" is mentioned in the 33ʳᵈ verse of Isaiah 37, and the 32ⁿᵈ verse of 2ⁿᵈ Kings 19, both under the title "Isaiah Predicts Judah's Deliverance." If you like, re-read chapter 5, to refresh your memory on this biblical event.

The 19ᵗʰ chapter of 2 Kings can be outlined as follow:
Verses 1 – 19   Hezekiah Seeks the Lord's Help

Verses 20 – 37   Isaiah Predicts Judah's Deliverance

The 37th chapter of Isaiah can be outlined as follow:
Verses 1 – 20   Hezekiah Seeks the Lord's Help
Verses 21 – 38   Isaiah Predicts Judah's Deliverance

Now, the Book of Isaiah has 66 chapters compared to 2 Kings which has 25 chapters. The author of 2nd Kings is unknown, but Scholars believe Jeremiah wrote 1st and 2nd Kings which were originally one book. It was written between 560 and 540 BC.

The Book of Isaiah is one of the most important books of the Old Testament. It is called "The Book of Salvation" which contains a collection of oracles, prophecies, and reports with the message of "salvation." According to Isaiah 1:1, it was written by the Prophet Isaiah. It was written between 701 and 681 BC.

The Prophet Isaiah was a Hebrew who lived in the Kingdom of Judah during the 8th BC. He was the son of Amoz who was born in Jerusalem. Isaiah name means "The Lord Saves." He accepted his calling as a prophet when he saw a vision in the year of King Uzziah's death. He was mainly called to prophesy to the Kingdom of Judah. The Kingdom of Judah was going through times of revival and rebellion. Isaiah begins his ministry during the same era of Amos, Hosea, and Micah.

Note of Interests: Amos prophesied during the reigns of King Uzziah and Jeroboam II of Israel; 760 – 755 BC. He claims that Israel will be carried away into exile as punishment for their sins against God. His prophecies came true when Assyrians conquers the Northern Kingdom. Hosea prophesied just before the destruction of Israel in 722 BC, during the reigns of Uzziah, Jotham, Ahaz, and Hezekiah; the kings of Judah. Micah prophecy was directly towards Jerusalem between 737 and 696 BC. His messages were concerning the future destruction of Jerusalem and Samaria; he rebuked the people of Judah for dishonesty and idolatry. Micah lived during the reign of Kings Jotham, Ahaz and Hezekiah of Judah. Micah also prophesied of Jesus' birth, Micah 5:3 – 5.

Isaiah spent most of his life in Jerusalem under King Hezekiah, Isaiah 37:1 – 2. He was married and had 2 sons named Shearjashub, and Mahershalalhashbaz; Isaiah 7:3 and Isaiah 8:3. Scholars believe during the reign of King Manasseh; the Prophet Isaiah met his death by being sawed in-half.

Note of Interests: The name "Shearjashub" which the Prophet Isaiah named his 1st born son means "A remnant shall return." It only appears once in the Bible. The name "Mahershalalhashbaz" means "He has made haste to the plunder." It appears twice in Isaiah 8, only. Mahershalalhashbaz is also counted as the longest name in the Bible. The NIV and NLT divide Isaiah's son names as follow:

1. Sheraijashub   -Shear – jashub
2. Mahershalalhashbaz   -Maher – shalal – hash – baz

Isaiah is best known for prophesying the coming of the Messiah Jesus Christ to mankind, Isaiah 7:14, Isaiah 9:1 – 7, Isaiah 11:1 – 10. Most Scholars believe Isaiah wrote chapters 1 – 39 in the Book of Isaiah with the remainder of the book authored by several other prophets. Isaiah definitely wrote about the history of the reign of King Uzziah, 2 Chronicles 26:22.

> **The rest of the events of Uzziah's**
> **reign, from beginning to end,**
> **are recorded by the prophet Isaiah son of Amoz.**
> 2 Chronicles 26:22 NLT

Note of Interests: King Uzziah name means "Yah is my strength." He is also known as Azariah recorded in 2 Kings. Uzziah was the 11th King of Judah, one of the sons of Amaziah, and has the 2nd longest tenure as Judah's king. Uzziah began to reign at age 16 and reigned for 52 years. The 1st 24 years of his reign were co-regent with his father, Amaziah. He was considered one of the good kings of Judah. Uzziah was later struck with leprosy for disobeying God, 2 Kings 15:2, 2 Chronicles 26:18 – 21. He entered the temple of God to burn incense. The priests were appointed to burn incense on the altar, only. When 80 priests tried to stop King Uzziah, he became angry at them. While he was at the altar of incense in the Lord's temple, leprosy broke out on his forehead. Jotham, his son, governed the people in his place. Uzziah lived in a separate palace until his death. King Uzziah is also mentioned as one of the ancestors of Joseph, Mary' husband, the mother of Jesus, Matthew 1:8 – 9.

The Book of Isaiah is the first of the Major Prophet Books in the Old Testament. Scholars widely accepted that the Book of Isaiah is rooted in a historical prophet named Isaiah. Scholars also believe that Isaiah did not write the entire Book of Isaiah.

The Book of Isaiah has 3 separate collections of oracles.

1. Chapters 1 – 39 contains the words of Isaiah.
2. Chapters 40 – 55 is the work of an anonymous exilic author.
3. Chapter 56 – 66 is the writing after the people return from exile.

Isaiah 37 read exactly like 2nd Kings 10. Remember, Hezekiah immediately went into the house of the Lord and prayed, upon hearing the words of the Assyrian's chief of staff. Hezekiah sent Eliakim, Shebna and the leading priest to the Prophet Isaiah, Isaiah 37: 1 – 2. Isaiah encourages Hezekiah with an unfavorable message from God concerning Sennacherib, Isaiah 37:5 – 7.

Sennacherib sent another message to King Hezekiah. He boasted, cursed, threatened and condemned the God of Israel, again. Hezekiah takes his troubles and the letter to God in prayer, Isaiah 37:14 – 20. Isaiah delivers God's message to King Hezekiah concerning King Sennacherib. He is given a promise that King Sennacherib of Assyrian will not besiege or invade, nor shoot an arrow at the city of Jerusalem, Isaiah 37:33 – 35.

Isaiah 37:33 reads:

Therefore,
thus saith the Lord concerning the king of Assyria,
He shall not come into this city,
nor shoot an arrow there,
nor come before it with shields,
nor cast a bank against it.
Isaiah 37:33 KJV

According to the last few verses of Isaiah 37, the Angel of the Lord killed 185,000 men of the Assyrian's army in one night. Afterward, Sennacherib fled home to Nineveh. While he was worshipping his god, 2 of his sons murdered him with a sword, verses 36 – 38. His son named Esarhaddon became king.

CHAPTER 12

Deadly Arrow

Their tongue is a deadly arrow; it speaks deceitfully.
With their mouths they all speak
cordially to their neighbors,
but in their hearts, they set traps for them.
Jeremiah 9:8 NIV

Jeremiah is viewed as one of the great prophets of Israel. He was also called the "weeping prophet." Jeremiah was weeping day and night at the thought of impending judgment for Judah's sins against God. He traveled among the people begging, pleading, and imploring them to turn from their wicked ways but in vain.

When Jeremiah's life is compared to the other prophets in the Bible, there is much more known about his life. He was born in a priestly family, the son of Hilkiah a Jewish priest from the town of Anathoth, 2 miles south of Jerusalem, and belonged to the tribe of Benjamin. God didn't permit Jeremiah to marry, Jeremiah 16:2.

It was around 627 BC, Jeremiah received his Godly calling while he was still a youth. Many Scholars believe it was between the age of 12 – 20. Jeremiah is the prophet that when God confirmed his calling, he put forth his hand and touched his mouth, Jeremiah 1:4 – 10. He prophesied about Jerusalem destruction and lived in the final days of the siege and destruction of the nation Judah by Babylonian. He was the last prophet that God sent to preach to the southern kingdom, the tribes of Judah and Benjamin.

Jeremiah told the people the destruction of Judah would occur because Israel had been unfaithful to the laws of the covenant and forsaken God by worshipping Baal. Jeremiah also condemned the people who were burning their children as offerings to Molech.

Note of Interests: The ancient god name "Molech" is mentioned 8 times in the Bible; it is also known as Moloch, Molek, Milcom or Malcam. The Canaanites worshiped it during the Old Testament era. The word "Canaanites" is used in general to refer to all the inhabitants of the land of Canaan which included 7 pagan tribes in Canaan; the Amorites, Canaanites, Girgashites, Hittites, Hivites, Jebusites, and Perizzites, Joshua 11:3. (**PS:** Little more details in the back of the book) Molech worship consisted of a living child being sacrificed by fire. The first time Molech is mentioned in the Bible is in Leviticus 18:21; the Lord commanded Israel not to participate in Molech worship and repeatedly instructed Israel to destroy the inhabitants that worshipped Molech. Even, Solomon was swayed by his Canaanite wives and built places of worship for Molech, 1 Kings 11:1 – 7. Molech worship occurred in the "high places," and "low valleys," 1 Kings 12:31 and 2 Kings 23:10. Despite the efforts of godly kings, the worship of Meloch wasn't abolished until Israel was taken in captivity by Babylon. The Babylonian religion believed in many gods, but none included human sacrifice. Meloch was a giant upright bronze statue with a bull's head with horns, adorned with a royal crown, seated on a throne with outstretched forearms to receive the child sacrifice.

Scholars believe that Jeremiah is the author of 1st and 2nd Kings, and Lamentations with the assistance of Baruch ben Neriah, his scribe. His ministry was active from the 13th year of King Josiah, the king of Judah until after the fall of Jerusalem and the destruction of Solomon's Temple in 587 BC. His ministry spanned over the reign of 5 kings of Judah; King Josiah, Jehoahaz, Jehoiakim, Jehoiachin, and Zedekiah.

Note of Interests: It was during the reign of Jehoiakim, the king of Judah, that he threw the scroll of Jeremiah in the fire; after Jehudi read it to the people around 605 BC, Jeremiah 36.

The Book of Jeremiah is the 2nd book of the Major Prophet Books, and the 24th book of the Old Testament. Jeremiah contains more words than any other book in the Bible, making it the longest book in the Bible with 52 chapters. The Book of Jeremiah has approximately 33,002 words. The next 2 books with the most words are Genesis with 32,046 words and Psalms with 30,147 words.

However, the Book of Isaiah, the 1ˢᵗ Major Prophet Book has the most chapters, a total of 66 chapters with 25,608 words. We all know, the Book of Psalms in the Bible has the most chapters; a total of 150 chapters, but it is considered one of the poetic books in the Bible.

The Book of Jeremiah was written between 630 and 580 BC. Jeremiah records the final prophecies to Judah. It warns Judah about their imminent destruction if the nation doesn't repent. Jeremiah called the nation to turn back to God, but they don't. The Book of Jeremiah can be outlined as follows.

1. Prophecies against Judah and Jerusalem, chapters 1 – 25
2. Narratives about Jeremiah, chapters 26 – 45
3. Prophecies against Foreign Nations, chapters 46 – 51
4. Historical Appendix, chapter 52

After the death of King Josiah who was the last righteous king, the nation of Judah had practically abandoned God and His commandments. The Prophet Jeremiah compares Judah to prostitutes. God had promised, He would judge idolatry severely, and Jeremiah was warning Judah that God's judgment was at hand. God had delivered Judah from destruction on numerous occasions, but His mercy for them was about to end.

The wicked and immoral behavior of God's once chosen people had reached its ultimate point. The gruesome punishment which their apostasy deserved was soon to be executed upon the reprobate nation.

The 9ᵗʰ chapter of Jeremiah has 26 verses, and can be outlined as follows:

1. Jeremiah Mourns for His People, verses 1 – 2
2. The Lord's Judgment for Disobedience, verses 3 – 9
3. Jeremiah Weeps for His People, verses 10 – 11
4. Forthcoming Ruin and Exile by the Lord, verses 12 – 16
5. Weeping in Jerusalem, verses 17 – 22
6. What the Lord Desire His People to Do, verses 23 – 26

The word "arrow" is embedded in the section titled "The Lord Judgment for Disobedience." The word "arrow" is in a verse that is one of the reasons the Lord gives Jeremiah for Judah imminent destruction. Beginning in verse 3 of this chapter, the Lord says the people mouths are full of lies. At verse 8, the Lord tells Jeremiah that the people say they want peace, but they are telling a deadly lie, like an arrow that strikes when you least expect it.

Jeremiah 9:8 reads:

For their tongues shoot lies like poisoned arrows.
They speak friendly words to their neighbors
while scheming in their heart to kill them.
Jeremiah 9:8 NLT

This section titled, "The Lord Judgment for Disobedience" ends with the Lord asking Jeremiah, "Should he not punish them for this? Should He not avenge himself against such a nation?" Jeremiah 9:9.

CHAPTER 13

A Mark for the Arrow

The words "a mark for the arrow" are recorded in Lamentations 3:12. The word "Lamentation" is defined as the passionate expression of grief, sorrow or sadness. It can be expressed by crying, howling, moaning, sobbing, wailing, or weeping.

> **He hath bent his bow and set me**
> **as a mark for the arrow.**
> Lamentations 3:12 KJV

The Book of Lamentations is a collection of poetic laments in the Bible written by Jeremiah around 586 BC. It echoes on what happened to Jerusalem. The Prophet Jeremiah reflects on the destruction of Jerusalem, and the Holy Temple followed by the Babylonian Exile. The destruction was by God because of the collective sins of His people.

Note of Interests: Jeremiah is also known as the "weeping prophet." He wrote Lamentations after the destruction of Jerusalem by the Babylonians. Jeremiah poured out his love-kindness and his tender-heartedness to God's people, as he expressed that disobedience to the Lord will result in tremendous anguish, hardship, and suffering.

The Book of Lamentations has 5 chapters, and each chapter is a lament with 22 verses, except for chapter 3. The 22 verses correspond to the 22 letters of the Hebrew alphabet. The first lines beginning with the 1st letter of the alphabet, the 2nd line with the 2nd letter, and so on. Chapter 3 has 66 verses, and each letter of the Hebrew alphabet begins 3 lines. The 5th lament is not acrostic but still has 22 lines.

Note of Interests: An acrostic is a poem or a form of writing in which the 1st letter of each line or paragraph spells out a word, message or the alphabet.

Lamentation 3:12 is the verse where the word "arrow" is mentioned under the Hebrew alphabet "Daleth." Daleth is the 4th letter of the Hebrew alphabet, and the other two verses that correspond with "Daleth" in Lamentations 3 are 10 and 11. The 22 letters of the Hebrew alphabet are listed below, along with the 3 verses that correspond to that particular alphabet in Lamentations 3.

Hebrew Alphabet	Corresponding Verses
1. Aleph	1 – 3
2. Beth	4 – 6
3. Gimel	7 – 9
4. Daleth	10 – 12

5.	He	13 – 15
6.	Waw/Vav	16 – 18
7.	Zayin	19 – 21
8.	Cheth	22 – 24
9.	Teth	25 – 27
10.	Yod	28 – 30
11.	Kaph	31 – 33
12.	Lamed	34 – 36
13.	Mem	37 – 39
14.	Nun	40 – 42
15.	Samek	43 – 45
16.	Pe	46 – 48
17.	Ayin	49 – 51
18.	Tsade	52 – 54
19.	Qoph	55 – 57
20.	Resh	58 – 60
21.	Sin/Shin	61 – 63
22.	Taw/Tav	64 – 66

The Book of Lamentations is customarily recited annually by Jews on the fast day of Tisha B'Av which is the 9th day in the month of Av, and it's considered the saddest day on the Jewish's calendar. They fast for 25 hours while mourning the destruction of Jerusalem and the Holy Temple. They are prohibited from 5 activities which are listed below; except if they are gravely ill which will be determined by a rabbi.

1. No eating or drinking
2. No washing or bathing
3. No application of creams or oils

4.   No wearing of shoes
5.   No marital sexual relations

In Christianity, the Book of Lamentations is usually read during Tenebrae of the Holy Triduum. Tenebrae is a religious service of Western Christianity held during the 3rd days, before Easter. Western Christianity will be readings, chanting, and singing from the Book of Lamentations during the Lenten religious service known as the Tenebrae.

Note of Interests: A triduum is a 3-day period of prayer that recalls the 3 days that Christ spent in the tomb, from Good Friday until Easter Sunday. Holy Thursday is the 1st night of the Triduum, Jesus washed his disciples' feet on this night. Good Friday, Jesus died on the cross, saving us from eternal damnation. Holy Saturday is the day that Jesus laid in the tomb. An Easter Vigil is held before dawn on Easter Sunday celebrating the resurrection of Jesus.

⸻

In the Church of England, the Book of Lamentations is read in the morning, and evening prayer on Monday and Tuesday of Holy Week, and at Evening Prayer on Good Friday. In the Coptic Orthodox Church, Lamentation 3 is chanted on the 12 hours of the Good Friday service, that commemorates the burial of Jesus.

The Book of Lamentations 5 chapters can be outlined as follows.

1. Chapter 1 -   A Lament on the Miserable End Sin on People

2. Chapter 2 - A Lament on God's Punishment and the People Miseries
3. Chapter 3 - A Lament on Jeremiah Personal Suffering
4. Chapter 4 - A Lament on the Ruin and Desolation of Jerusalem
5. Chapter 5 - A Lament for God' Mercy and A Prayer of Repentance

The 3rd chapter of Lamentations is Jeremiah's lament on personal suffering. This chapter can be outlined as follow.

1. Jeremiah's Sorrows, verses 1 – 18
2. Jeremiah's Hope, verses 19 – 39
3. Jeremiah's Cried Out and Pray, verses 40 – 66

Beginning at Lamentation 3:1, Jeremiah has seen much affliction because the Lord is punishing Jerusalem for their sins. Jeremiah is also suffering during this time, verses 1 – 3.

Jeremiah's suffering included sickness, broken bones, being hungry, and feeling alone. Jeremiah mentioned that the Lord would not let him escape from his hardships nor ease his suffering or answer his prayers, verses 7 – 9.

In verses 11 – 13 of Lamentations 3, Jeremiah revealed how he feels about what happened in his life. He feels as if the Lord laid in wait and then attacked him as a bear or lion. He feels as if the Lord has torn him into pieces leaving him helpless, and desolate. And finally, he feels as though, he was a target that the Lord carefully aim and shot an arrow straight through his heart; severely wounding him.

**He drew his bow and made me
the target for his arrows.
He pierced my heart with arrows from his quiver.**
Lamentations 3:12 – 13 NIV

Note of Interests: Lamentations 3:12 in the NIV and NLT Bibles, the word "arrow" has an "s," but not KJV, NKJV or AKJV.

In the remainder of this section titled "Jeremiah's Sorrow," Jeremiah mentioned that the other prophets mocked and ridiculed him daily. His life has been turned upside-down by the Lord. His teeth are broken from eating gravel, and he is covered in dust and ashes.

Jeremiah goes on to say; he had forgotten what happiness feels like, peace looks like, and what prosperity is. He has lost his hope in the Lord, verse 18. In verses 19 – 39, Jeremiah begins to express hope, and then at the end of Lamentations 3, Jeremiah prays to the Lord, verses 40 – 66.

CHAPTER 14

The Lord's Arrow

In Zechariah 9:14 is where the word "arrow" is embedded among 30 words in the NLT, and 33 words in the KJV. It is describing how the Lord will defend his people.

The Lord will appear above his people; his arrows will fly like lightning! The Sovereign Lord will sound the ram's horn and attack like a whirlwind from the southern desert. Zechariah 9:14 NLT

And the Lord shall be seen over them, and his arrow shall go forth as the lightning: and the Lord God shall blow the trumpet, and shall go with whirlwinds of the south. Zechariah 9:14 KJV

The name "Zechariah" means "God remembered." Zechariah prophecies took place during the reign of Darius the Great. Darius the Great was the last king of the Achaemenid Empire of Persia. Haggai and Malachi were prophets of the Persian period, also. The Achaemenid Period lasted from 450 – 330 BC.

Note of Interests: Haggai was a prophet during the building of the 2nd Temple in Jerusalem. He is known for his prophecy that commanded the Jews to finish rebuilding the Temple after it had been placed on hold for 18 years. The Old Testament ended with the prophecies of Malachi. He prophesied at a time of great disorder among the people and priests. He rebuked the people for intermarriage with an idolatrous people. He reminds Israel of God's love.

Zechariah was a prophet from the Kingdom of Judah. He encouraged the remnant, who had recently returned to Jerusalem from exile. He strengthened their faith in God and helped them to conform to the law of God while motivating them to build the temple. Zechariah was also a priest because of his family lineage. Zechariah's grandfather was a priest named Iddo who returned with Zerubbabel back to Jerusalem.

Note of Interests: Zerubbabel led the 1st group of Jews who returned to Jerusalem, about 42,360 people between 538 and 520 BC. He also laid the foundation of the 2nd Temple in Jerusalem soon after their return.

Among the Minor Prophet Books, the Book of Zechariah contains the most messianic passage of scripture about the Messiah. The book declares the 1st coming of the Messiah who would be riding on a donkey, Zechariah 9:9. The book mentions Jesus betrayal in Zechariah 11:12, and Jesus' crucifixion is mentioned in Zechariah 12:10. The Book of Zechariah also describes the 2nd Coming of Jesus Christ descending from heaven the same way He left in Acts 1:11; in the clouds.

Zechariah the prophet is considered the author of the Book of Zechariah which was written after the return of Israel from Babylon captivity. Scholars believe Zechariah wrote chapters 1 – 8 around 520 BC before the temple was built; then around 480 BC, after the temple was built, Zechariah wrote chapters 9 – 14.

The Book of Zechariah has 14 chapters which contain 8 visions, 4 messages, and 2 oracles. It's the 11th book of the 12 Minor Prophet Books and the next to last book in the Old Testament; the 38th book.

The Book of Zechariah can be outlined as follow.

Chapters 1 – 8
These chapters recall Israel's history. Zechariah records a series of 8 visions he had one after another, in the same night. He encourages the Israelites to reinstate the priesthood and religious laws that were neglected during the 70-year exile. Zechariah gives hope about the coming Messiah, Jesus Christ, who will set up His throne and rule as the Lord Almighty, the High Priest, who will offer up the perfect sacrifice for the sins of the world, Zechariah 6:12 – 13.

Chapters 9 – 14
These chapters consist of two "Oracles." The 1st Oracle is in Zechariah, chapters 9 – 11. The 1st Oracle begins with a

prophecy against the Syrians. It stressed to Israel to expect success in all their struggles. It mentions the coming and rejection of the Messiah. The 2nd Oracle is in Zechariah, chapters 12 – 14. It points out the glories that await Israel in "latter day." It mentions the final conflict and triumph of God's kingdom. It speaks on the punishment and judgment on Israel's neighboring enemies.

The 9th chapter of Zechariah has 17 verses. It is divided into the following subjects.

1. Israel's Enemies will be Punished, verses 1 – 8
2. The Lord Speaks about the Coming Kings, verses 9 – 10
3. The Lord Promises to Rescue the Captives, verses 11 – 13
4. The Lord Will Protect His People, verses 14 – 17

Zechariah 9:1 – 8 mentions a series of judgments announced against the nations surrounding Israel, and verse 8 promises deliverance to God's people. Zechariah 9:9 – 10 mentions Christ's 1st and 2nd return. In verses 11 – 13, Zechariah speaks on the Lord's promises to rescue the captives, and his return to establish His universal kingdom. According to Zechariah 9:14 – 17, the Lord their God will protect and empower his people. The word "arrow" appears in Zechariah 9:14 in the 1st Oracle from the Lord which begins at Zechariah 9:1.

Zechariah 9:14 reads:

Then the Lord will appear over them;
his arrow will flash like lightning.
The Sovereign Lord will sound the trumpet;

he will march in the storms of the south,
and the Lord Almighty will shield them.
Zechariah 9:14 NIV

Biblical scholars believe this verse is saying; the Lord will reveal himself as he encourages and protects his people. The Lord's arrow of judgment shall go forth like lightning. He will inflict punishment upon Israel's enemies suddenly, like lightning flash. The priests will blow the trumpet as a signal for war. The whirlwinds of the south were considered the most destructive, and this is the way the Lord will come upon the enemies of Israel, sweeping them away with overwhelming force.

A READER'S QUESTION

This new section just dropped in my spirit at 0613 on January 14, 2017, titled <u>A Reader's Question</u>.

An individual asked me the following question:
Do you ever see your books being a movie someday?

<u>The Answer:</u>
Umh, a movie? No, but maybe a television, or radio program; or a biblical book club. The Apostle Paul wrote in Philippians 4:13, "I can do all thing through Christ who gives me strength." Therefore, I'm saying all things are possible with Father God.

In all thy ways acknowledge him,
and He shall direct thy paths.
Proverbs 3:6

AUTHOR'S CLOSING REMARKS

I learnt some beauties and trues about an "arrow" from writing this book, and the reading assignment. An arrow was 1ˢᵗ made from reeds, bamboo or wood. The word "arrow" and "arrows" in the Bible are used figuratively in Deuteronomy 32:23, Deuteronomy 32:42, Psalms 144:6, Zechariah 9:14.

The King of Babylon used arrows in the practice of seeking knowledge; foretelling the future, Ezekiel 21:21. The word arrows are often used as a symbol of tribulation inflicted by God, Job 6:4, Psalms 38:2, Deuteronomy 32:23. The word "arrow" and "arrows" are used to indicate false testimony in Proverbs 25:18, bitter words in Psalms 64:3, and sudden danger, Psalms 91:5. In conclusion, the words "arrow" and "arrows" are only found in the Old Testament.

If you like, feel free to add to the beauties and trues about an "arrow."

_____

_____

_____

_____

_____

_____

_____

_____

PS: I much confess. The reading assignment in Chapter 8; I haven't finished reading it, yet, as of 01/15/2019; a month later. I'm so off course. . . . . . . Father God, PLEASE forgive me, and strengthen me, and help me finish this assignment in Jesus' Name! Amen.

Pray for the Ministry . . . May the "LORD of Peace," give you His Peace.

Dr. Vanessa

REFERENCES

Chapter 1 Arrow
1. Wikipedia, The Free Encyclopedia: https://en.wikipedia.org/wiki/Arrow
2. BibleGateway: https://www.biblegateway.com

Chapter 2 The Stone Ezel
1. BibleGateway: https://www.biblegateway.com

Chapter 3 Jehu's Arrow
1. BibleGateway: https://www.biblegateway.com
2. Wikipedia, The Free Encyclopedia: https://en.wikipedia.org/wiki/Jehu

Chapter 4 Jehoash Shot an Arrow
1. Wikipedia, The Free Encyclopedia: https://en.wikipedia.org/wiki/Jehoash
2. BibleGateway: https://www.biblegateway.com

Chapter 5 Nor Shoot an Arrow
1. BibleGateway: https://www.biblegateway.com
2. Jacksonville Theology Seminary

3. Wikipedia, The Free Encyclopedia: https://en.wikipedia.org/wiki/Hezekiah

Chapter 6 No Arrow Can Make Him Flee
1. BibleGateway: https://www.biblegateway.com
2. Wikipedia, The Free Encyclopedia: https://en.wikipedia.org/wiki/Leviathan
3. Jacksonville Theology Seminary

Chapter 7 Make Ready Their Arrow
1. BibleGateway: https://www.biblegateway.com

Chapter 8 God Shall Shoot
1. Wikipedia, The Free Encyclopedia: https://en.wikipedia.org/wiki/Psalms

Chapter 9 Arrow that Flies
1. BibleGateway: https://www.biblegateway.com
2. Wikipedia, The Free Encyclopedia: https://en.wikipedia.org/wiki/Psalm_91

Chapter 10 A Sharp Arrow
1. Wikipedia, The Free Encyclopedia: https://en.wikipedia.org/wiki/Proverbs
2. BibleGateway: https://www.biblegateway.com
3. Jacksonville Theology Seminary

Chapter 11 Repetition
1. BibleGateway: https://www.biblegateway.com
2. Jacksonville Theology Seminary

Chapter 12 Deadly Arrow
1. BibleGateway: https://www.biblegateway.com

Chapter 13 A Mark for the Arrow
1. BibleGateway: https://www.biblegateway.com
2. Wikipedia, The Free Encyclopedia: https://en.wikipedia.org/wiki/Book_of_Lamentations

Chapter 14 The Lord's Arrow
1. BibleGateway:https://www.biblegateway.com
2. Wikipedia, The Free Encyclopedia: https://en.wikipedia.org/wiki/Book_of_Zechariah
3. Wikipedia, The Free Encyclopedia: https://en.wikipedia.org/wiki/Zerubbabel

ANSWERS & INFORMATION SECTION

Chapter 2
Jonathan shot 3 arrows, 1 Samuel 20:20.

Chapter 6
There are 5 Poetic Books in the Bible located in the Old Testament. They are Job, Psalms, Proverbs, Ecclesiastes, and the Song of Solomon.

Chapter 10
Proverbs 3:5 - 6

Chapter 12
The father of the "Canaanites" was Canaan a son of Ham, and the grandson of Noah. Canaan was the recipient of the "Curse of Ham. Ham, the son of Noah, saw his father nakedness and told his two brothers; Shem and Japheth. Shem and Japheth walked backward in the tent and covered their father nakedness, Genesis 9:20 - 28. When Noah learned what his youngest son, Ham had done, he cursed his son, Canaan. The 7 listed tribes/nations below are from Canaan descendants.

Amorites were very tall people. The 1st dynasty of Babylon was Amorite between 1830 – 1550 BC. Sihon and Og in the Bible were Amorite kings that dwell east of the Jordan River. They sacrificed their young infants to Molech.

Canaanites were more corrupt than the others; their worship entailed both heterosexual and homosexual ceremonies.

Girgashites were utterly immoral and corrupt who was in possession of the land of Canaan east of the Sea of Galilee. They were a branch of the family of the Hivites.

Hittites were very aggressive. Solomon had Hittite wives, 1 Kings 1:1. Esau married 2 Hittite women; Judith and Basemath in which his parents, Isaac and Rebekah weren't pleased with, Genesis 26:34 – 35.

Hivites were villager people, deceitful, and unwarlike. The Gibeonites were Hivites who deceived Joshua, Joshua 9:3.

Jebusites were combative people. They inhabitant the city that would later be named Jerusalem, Joshua 18:28.

Perizzites dwelt in unwalled cities, and their name means "rural people."

OTHER BOOKS BY THE AUTHOR:

From the Pew to the Pulpit   Published: 08/29/2007

Isaiah 26:3-4 "Perfect Peace"   Published: 09/07/2010

Isaiah 26:3-4 "Perfect Peace" The   Published: 02/13/2012
Last Single Digit

Isaiah 26:3-4 "Perfect Peace III"   Published: 10/24/2012
Silver and Gold

Isaiah 26:3-4 "Perfect Peace IV"   Published: 04/10/2013
The Kingdom Number

Isaiah 26:3-4 "Perfect Peace V"   Published: 09/06/2013
2541

Isaiah 26:3-4 "Perfect Peace VI"   Published: 02/28/2014
Zacchaeus

Isaiah 26:3-4 "Perfect Peace VII"   Published: 10/29/2014
Eleven

Isaiah 26:3-4 "Perfect Peace VIII" Published: 05/22/2015
Prayer

Isaiah 26:3-4 "Perfect Peace IX"   Published: 10/26/2015
Sixteen

Printed in the United States
By Bookmasters